Cornelius Kirsche

Black-Scholes Formula: A Walkthrough

GRIN Verlag

Bibliografische Information der Deutschen Nationalbibliothek:

Die Deutsche Bibliothek verzeichnet diese Publikation in der Deutschen National-
bibliografie; detaillierte bibliografische Daten sind im Internet über http://dnb.d-
nb.de/ abrufbar.

Imprint:

Copyright © 2012 GRIN Verlag GmbH
Druck und Bindung: Books on Demand GmbH, Norderstedt Germany
ISBN: 978-3-656-25952-7

This book at GRIN:

http://www.grin.com/en/e-book/197990/black-scholes-formula-a-walkthrough

GRIN - Your knowledge has value

Der GRIN Verlag publiziert seit 1998 wissenschaftliche Arbeiten von Studenten, Hochschullehrern und anderen Akademikern als eBook und gedrucktes Buch. Die Verlagswebsite www.grin.com ist die ideale Plattform zur Veröffentlichung von Hausarbeiten, Abschlussarbeiten, wissenschaftlichen Aufsätzen, Dissertationen und Fachbüchern.

Visit us on the internet:

http://www.grin.com/

http://www.facebook.com/grincom

http://www.twitter.com/grin_com

Master of International Management

Black-Scholes Formula: A Walkthrough

Cornelius Kirsche

(Master of International Management)

TABLE OF CONTENTS

LIST OF FORMULAS

1. INTRODUCTION

"The most influential development in terms of impact on finance practice was the Black-Scholes model for option pricing." – Robert Merton

Financial derivates found their way into the financial markets already hundreds of years ago. With the opening of the Chicago Board Options Exchange (CBOE) in 1973, they successfully established themselves in the market. Ever since, it is not possible to imagine a financial world without derivates (Balmer, 2002). Options build up one major type of financial derivates. With the opening of the CBOE, option trading has exponentially become popular in American securities markets. However, option pricing theory was still far off from being any precise. In fact, the question has always been on how to value options in a world where the underlying share was fluctuating (Cox, Ross & Rubinstein, 1979). The academics have also started to participate in this issue, believing that if they would be able to mathematically describe the emotional confidence of investors or traders, they would be able to solve the problem of how to value options. Hence, early econometric models kept on adding various parameters and factor to a mathematical formula in order to find the key to success – a problem to which its solution was later worth the Nobel Prize (French, 1983). However, it was Fischer Black and Myron Scholes who have published their groundbreaking findings in 1973 that revolutionized many aspects of option pricing today. According to Dan French, professor of Finance at Texas A&M University, "the Black-Scholes model, which was the first to define option pricing in equilibrium, is probably the most widely publicized and extensively tested of the probability-based models". The formula, which brought Scholes and Merton the Nobel Prize in 1997, was also valid and used in the real world by traders who soon imagined having the ultimate tool for making money (Balmer, 2002).

1

2. FROM THE BASICS TO THE PARITY

"The financial markets generally are unpredictable. So that one has to have different scenarios..."

- George Soros

2.1 PUT AND CALL OPTIONS

When speaking of options, all economical text books describe them as granting the buyer of a call option the right to buy the underlying financial asset at a fixed price, and on the other hand, to give the buyer of a put option the right to sell the underlying financial asset at a given price. In both cases, parties can either gain or lose money through a fluctuation in the price of the underlying (Damodaran, 2001). Option prices reflect the intrinsic value of the option, plus any additional amount over its intrinsic value, where the intrinsic value is considered to be the difference in the strike price and the stock price. This addition is known as the time premium. Further, when dealing with options, it is important to understand that both put and call options have a fixed expiration date. The owner of an option has the right to execute the option up until the expiration date. However, there are differences between an American option and a European option. The American option is exercised at any time prior to –and at the expiration date. With a European option, the option can only be exercised on the expiration date itself (Fabozzi & Modigliani, 2009).

Next to the ordinary buying or selling of call and put options, certain combinations exist, which in their nature fall back on the put-call parity, a theory which also finds its relevance in the Black-Scholes formula. However, looking at two wide-spread examples of option combinations, the author wants to start with the so-called covered call strategy. This rather conservative strategy is simultaneously buying equity and writing a call on the same share. Here, if the share price increases, the investor makes profit out of his share. If, on the opposite, the share price drops, the loss in the equity can be absorbed by the written call. A second combination is called the protective-put strategy. In this example, the investor buys the share in combination with buying a put option on the same underlying. Here, the investor may want to protect the value of the underlying against the risk of a decline in market value. As a result of the two approaches, the investor gets the same returns from the two possible strategies. Hence, a relationship exists, in showing that both options yield the same result (Jaffe, Ross & Westerfield, 2002).

2.2 PUT-CALL PARITY

In fact, this relationship is called the put-call parity.

Formula 1

$$\text{Price of underlying equity} + \text{Price of put} = \text{Price of call} + \text{Present value of exercise price}$$

Looking at the formula (*Formula 1*), there are now two ways to buy a protective put. The investor may either buy a put and buy the underlying share, in which the total cost would be the share price and the price of the put, or the investor can buy a call and buy a zero-coupon bond simultaneously. In the latter case, the costs would be the zero-coupon bond, which is equal to the present value of the exercise price, and the price of the call. There are a few assumptions that are important to this relationship, being that the put and call must have the same exercise price and expiration date and so does the maturity of the zero-coupon bond.

Formula 2

$$\text{Price of underlying equity} = \text{Price of call} - \text{Price of put} + \text{Present value of exercise price}$$

Rearranging the formula, one can understand that buying the underlying share can be exactly replicated in buying a call, selling a put and buying a zero-coupon bond. The author will refer back to this fundamental relationship, when dealing with the results of the Black-Scholes formula (Jaffe, Ross & Westerfield, 2002).

3. BLACK-SCHOLES – AN OPTION PRICING MODEL
3.1 ASSUMPTIONS OF THE MODEL AND ITS INFLUENCING FACTORS

The previous sections aimed to provide an overview of the basics when dealing with options. The Black-Scholes model requires being equipped with those fundamentals. The Black-Scholes model is one which is based on probabilities, as it determines the value of an option upon the probability that the share will be situated above exercise price on the specific expiration date. As with many models, also the Black-Scholes falls back on given conditions, being (Black & Scholes, 1973):

1. A constant risk-free interest rate
2. Share price changes are log-normally distributed
3. No dividends occur
4. Options can only be exercised at maturity date
5. No transactions costs occur
6. Borrowings are unlimited

3

If the above conditions are fulfilled, the value of an option solely depends on five factors: price of the stock, exercise price of the option, time to expiration of the option, risk-free rate and the expected variance of the distribution, or the standard deviation of the stock price. In the following, those five factors are abbreviated for the calculations as follows (Fabozzi & Modigliani, 2009):

C = call option price

S = current stock price

X = strike price

r = short-term risk-free interest rate over the life of the option

t = time remaining to the expiration date (as a fraction of one year)

s = standard deviation of the share price

N = the cumulative probability density

The first four factors can be observed whereas the standard deviation of the share price falls back on estimations. Before actually discussing on the formula, the key intuition behind the Black-Scholes model is worth emphasizing a bit further. What the Black-Scholes model shows is the exact price for an option, by imposing certain assumptions as well as using arbitrage arguments, to compute the theoretical value or provide of a European call option (Jaffe, Ross & Westerfield, 2002).

3.2 THE BLACK-SCHOLES FORMULA

The Black-Scholes formula is known to be (Bhattacharya, 1980):

Formula 3

$$C = SN(d_1) - Xe^{-rt}N(d_2)$$

Additionally, d_1 and d_2 can be further broken down into:

Formula 4

$$d_1 = \frac{\ln(\frac{S}{X}) + (r + \frac{\sigma^2}{2})t}{\sigma\sqrt{t}}$$

and

Formula 5

$$d_2 = d_1 - \sigma\sqrt{t}$$

Taking a closer look at the components of the formula, the author wants to start with *Formula 3*, stated above. Here, the cumulative probability density of d_1 is multiplied with the current stock price. For the second part of the Black-Scholes formula, the term Xe^{-rt} simply descripts

4

the present value of the strike price X. Further, the term e^{-rt} is the continous compounding discount factor for the present value calculation. The present value of an option, which was just explained to be Xe^{-rt}, will consequently be its expected value at maturity date continously discounted at risk-free rate. This present value is then multiplied with the cumulative probability density of d_2.

As an additional insight, since a hedged portfolie can be created with a combination of buying the underlying, and selling an option, the profit with e.g. an increase in share price will be exactly counterbalanced with the decline in the value of the sold option. Now, the Black-Scholes model states, that if such a hedged condition can be constructed for a portfolio where the value does not change, the portfolio can be regarded as riskless.

Further, given the price at any time, the logarithm of the price at a later stage is normally disttributed. For that reason, the Black-Scholes formula is lognormal; including the *In* in the formula (French, 1983). The variable t occurs in both the d_1 and d_2 formulas. This does not reflect days, as it does in various other financial models or ratios, but is rather calculated as a fraction of one (Macbeth & Merville, 1979). Additionally, in the real world, the standard deviation σ is rather referred to as the implied volatility of the option. Following the formulas for d_1 and d_2, the results need to be looked up in a cumulative probability table for the Standard Normal Distribution, in order to arrive at the $N(d_1)$ and $N(d_2)$ variables. As we look at the formula, there are no variables for cash distributions such as dividends or transaction costs, which the author has discussed previously as being one key assumption of the model. (Black & Scholes, 1973).

3.3 THE BLACK-SCHOLES FORMULA IN PRACTICE

The author first wants to illustrate the above explained formula using a fictional examples. Afterwards, the Black-Scholes model will be applied to a real world case.

3.3.1 Fictional Example

What is the price of a call option, given the following values:

$S = 80$, $R = 5\%$, $\sigma = 0.4068$, $X = 80$ and $t = 180/365$ days

$$d_1 = \frac{\ln(\frac{80}{80}) + (0.05 + \frac{0.4068^2}{2})180/365}{0.4068\sqrt{180/365}}$$

$$d_1 = 0.2297$$

$$d_2 = 0.2297 - 0.4068\sqrt{180/365}$$

$$d_2 = -0.058$$

Now where we have derived the values for d_1 and d_2, one can now substitude the values into the basic Black-Scholes formula.

$$C = 80*N(0.2297) - Xe^{-rt}N(-0.058)$$

Using the Standard Distribution Table, the $N(d_1)$ and $N(d_2)$ values can be derived as being: $N(d_1) = 0.5908$ and $N(d_2) = 0.4769$.

However, the present value of the strike price still needs to be calculated beforehand:

$$PV(X) = 80*e^{-(0.05)*(180/365)}$$

$$PV(X) = 78.05$$

Further, all variable are known, and the formula can be finally solved:

$$C = 80*0.5908 - 78.05*0.4769$$

$$C = \$10.05$$

Hence, the value of the call for the details mentioned above is $10.05 (Allen, Brealey & Myers, 2007).

3.3.2 General Electric Example

In a second example, the author uses the General Electric Share with actual figures. An overview of the infromation required is shown in Table 1 and Table 2 (Schuster, 2011).

Table 1

Call Detail			Put Detail	
Price	Implied Volatility	Strike	Implied Volatility	Price
$7,32	0%	13	50%	$0,03
$5,35	51%	15	40%	$0,05
$4,35	43%	16	35%	$0,07
$3,38	36%	17	30%	$0,10
$2,44	30%	18	28%	$0,19
$1,59	26%	19	25%	$0,36
$0,89	23%	20	23%	$0,69
$0,41	21%	21	22%	$1,23
$0,17	21%	22	21%	$1,99
$0,05	20%	23	21%	$2,88
$0,01	20%	24	24%	$3,85
$0,00	21%	25	31%	$4,88
Expiration Date: 16.7.11				
US 3-month Treasury Bill: 0,01%				

Table 2

Closing		Returns		Historical		
Date	Price	1-Day	10-Day	1-Month	2-Month	3-Month
10.5.11	$20,30	$0,01	$0,01	18,30%	20,24%	21,16%

In order to be consistent, the author will transfor the relevent data form the table above, into the format used in the first example of the paper. Therefore, S = 20.0 , R = 0.01%, σ = 0.43, X = 16 and t = 67/365 days.

The value of a call can now be calculated following the explained structure.

Hence:

$$d_1 = \frac{\ln(\frac{20}{16}) + (0.0001 + \frac{0.43^2}{2})67/365}{0.43\sqrt{67/365}}$$

$d_1 = 1.384255$

$d_2 = 1.384255 - 0.43\sqrt{67/365}$

$d_2 = 1.200026$

In a second step, the cumulative statistical values need to be assigned to the the the d-values; here, $N(d_1) = 0.9162$ and $N(d_2) = 0.8849$.

Before coming to the final step of the Balck-Scholes, the present value of the strike price needs to be calculated for the stike price of 16.

$PV(X) = 16 * e^{-(0.01)*(67/365)}$

$PV(X) = 15.97$

Finally, the call value can be derived using the orignal Black-Scholes formula.

$C = 20.3 * 0.9162 - 15.97 * 0.8849$

$C = \$4.46$

What the two examples should underline is to show that both in theory but also in practice, the Black-Scholes formula is relevant. However, the power of such tools is not only in the nature of looking at models separately, but combining different frameworks effectively. In fact, referring back to the previous mentioned put-call parity, one can now derive the value of a put, by using the above calculated call price as well as rearranging the put-call parity model. Assuming the same strike price:

Price of the Put = Price of the Call + PV(X) – S

Price of the Put = 4.446 + 15.97 – 20.30

Price of the Put = \$0.12

The value of the put is comparably low. Nevertheless, imagining that the current share price is \$20.30 and the put option would allow you to sell the underlying equity at 16, the owner of this put option will not execute it as long as the strike price is still below the share price.

3.4 EXCURSION TO THE GREEKS

The `Greeks´ are worth mentioning when dealing with options and their valuation. In general, they measure the rate of change in the value of a call or put option. Since the formula is extremely complex and would require a separate paper itself to explain it, the author will focus on giving an overview on what the Greeks stand for. The most frequently cited letters are Delta, Gamma, Theta and Vega.

In detail, Delta measures the rate of change in the value of a specific option, with respect to the change in the underlying share price. Here, the Delta for e.g. a call option is always between 0 and 1, whereas a put option is represented by values between 0 and -1. As an example, if the Delta is 0.5, this means that the value of the call increases by 0.50€ for every 1€ increase in the underlying equity (Deacon & Faseruk, 2000).

The Gamma, on the other hand, is a measure for the change of delta with respect to the underlying equity. To simplify the theory, we consider a call option that has a Gamma of 0.03 and a delta of 0.7, if the share price increases by 1.00€, the delta of this option will grow by 0.03 to 0.73. The Gamma further has additional characteristics like that it is small when options are heavily out of the money or when the share price is very high compared to the exercise price of a put option (Jaffe, Ross & Westerfield, 2002).

The next letter that is being discussed is the Theta. The Theta focuses in the sensitivity in the value of an option, with respect to their time to maturity. The value of Theta will always be negative since an option loses value as it reaches the exercise date.

Finally, Vega describes the sensitivity of an option with respect to its change in volatility. Here, the closest relation to the Black-Scholes can be found since the implied volatility can be derived by using the Black-Scholes formula (Deacon & Faseruk, 2000).

4. CONCLUSION

The Black-Scholes formula has grown universal acceptance since the formula helps to understand whether an option is priced with a fair value, taking into account volatility, risk-free return with respect to the underlying share price and a certain strike price; all this, using a model which is easy to use in times of excel spreadsheets and sophisticated financial calculators (Gibson, 2003). Nevertheless, one is still dealing with a mathematical framework which does not respect human intuition and rational thinking. Having said this, the author wants to roll out on a case that is related to a failure of the Black-Scholes model. In 1995, Myron Scholes and Robert Merton joint forces and started their own business called Long-Term Capital Management (LTCM); based on their mathematical formula, they were about to

trade on a scale which was never seen before. Since Scholes was rewarded the Nobel Prize, investors seemed to even be honored to invest into the new business. This made it possible to raise a capital of $5 billion to invest. The knowledge and the experience of Scholes and Merton eventually paid off (Marsh & Kobayashi, 2000). In a BBC documentation, Roger Lowenstein who is an American financial journalist and writer said: "LTCM started out with three truly fabulous years. The first year they made 20% and that was after the partners had collected handsome fees. The second year they returned 43% to their investors, the third year another 41%" (Horizon, 1999). However, as with all mathematical and theoretical frameworks, they struggle if the unexpected happens. With the financial crisis in Russia in 1998 the Russian Government defaulted on their bonds. The markets reacted extremely nervous and investors started to sell European and Japanese bonds in order to invest in US treasury bonds. A great proportion of LTCM's investment strategy was based on exactly those Russian bonds. The formula could not calculate with events that occurred randomly. Further, the property prices in Thailand collapsed, which resulted in a wave of uncertainty going through Asia. The calculations at LTCM assumed that markets will return to normal in a bit of time. In this situation, LTCM took up another $100 billion for new investments. However, four days after the default of Russia, LTCM has dropped $500 million in a single day (Horizon, 1999). Soon after, LTCM declared bankruptcy. As many major Wall Street investment houses have trusted LTCM with their money, the Federal Reserve has ordered a bail-out. Otherwise, the market would have been horribly shaking and major banks and investment houses might have lost millions (BusinessWeek, 1998).

What the author wants to show with that case is, that even if certain models were granted a Nobel Prize, they still need to be handled with care and in rare cases do they substitute rational or emotional reasoning of human beings. However, the Black-Scholes formula can be regarded as being a very powerful tool in understanding and calculating option values. Which was in previous times rather a case of magic or uncertainty, can now be derived very precisely. The beauty of the formula will, nevertheless, still encourage millions of traders or investors to use the formula on a daily basis.

REFERENCE LIST

Allen, R., Brealey, R. A., & Myers, S. C. (2007). *Principles of corporate finance*. (Ninth ed.). McGraw-Hill.

Balmer, T. (2002). *Option Pricing Theory* (Diploma dissertation). University of Zurich. Retrieved from www.bf.uzh.ch/publikationen/diplomarbeiten/ lbdipl_balmer_thomas.pdf

Bhattacharya, M. (1980). EMPIRICAL PROPERTIES OF THE BLACK-SCHOLES FORMULA UNDER IDEAL CONDITIONS. *Journal Of Financial & Quantitative Analysis*, 15(5), 1081-1105.

Black, F., & Scholes, M. (1973). The Pricing of Options and Corporate Liabilities. *Journal Of Political Economy*, 81(3), 637.

BusinessWeek (1998, November 9). WHO'S WATCHING THE HEDGE FUNDS?. *BusinessWeek*. p. 186.

Cox, J. C., Ross, S. A., & Rubinstein, M. (1979). Option pricing: A simplified approach. *Journal of Financial Economics*

Damodaran, A. (2001). *Corporate finance*. (Second ed.). USA: John Wiley & Sons.

Deacon, C. G., & Faseruk, A. (2000). AN EXAMINATION OF THE GREEKS (GREEK SYMBOLS) FROM THE BLACK SCHOLES OPTION PRICING MODEL. *Journal Of Financial Management & Analysis*, 13(1), 50.

Fabozzi, F. J., & Modigliani, F. (2009). *Capital markets*. (Fourth ed.). New Jersey: Pearson Education.

French, D. W. (1983). BLACK-SCHOLES vs. KASSOUF OPTION PRICING: AN EMPIRICAL COMPARISON. *Journal Of Business Finance & Accounting*, 10(3), 395-408.

Gibson, N. (2003). *Essential finance*. (First ed., pp. 50-51). Bloomberg Press.

Horizon. (Producer). (1999, December 2). *The Midas Formula* [Television broadcast]. London: British Broadcasting Corporation.

Jaffe, J., Ross, S. A., & Westerfield, R. W. (2002). *Corporate finance*. (Sixth ed.). Punta Gorda: Mcgraw-Hill College.

Lowenstein, R. When Genius Failed: The Rise and Fall of Long-Term Capital Management. Random House, New York, 2000.

Macbeth, J. D., & Merville, L. J. (1979). An Empirical Examination of the Black-Scholes Call Option Pricing Model. *Journal Of Finance*, 34(5), 1173-1186.

Marsh, T., & Kobayashi, T. (2000). The Contributions of Professors Fischer Black, Robert
      Merton and Myron Scholes to the Financial Services Industry. *International Review*
      Of Finance, 1(4), 295.

Schuster, T. (2011). *Intermediate Financial Management* [PowerPoint slides]. Retrieved from
      http://www.care.iubh.de/